Tony Harrison

THE FIRE GAP

A POEM WITH TWO TAILS

BLOODAXE BOOKS

MCMLXXXV

and I hacked off her hooded head.
Then I lopped this 'laithly worm'
and sliced the creature into nine
reptilian lengths that I saw squirm
as if still one connected spine.
The gaps between the bits I'd lopped
seemed supple snake though made of air
so that I wondered where life stopped
and if death started, where?
Since that time I've never killed
any snake that's come my way
between the wild land and the tilled
where I walk every day

gap, cereals, savannah.
Best keep to my land if you're wise.
Once you cross my boundary line
the Bible-belters exorcise
all traces of the serpentine,
from Satan plain to demon drink,
the flesh you're blamed for keeping hot,
all earth-embracing snakes that slink
whether poisonous or not;
the fairy, pacifist, the Red,
maybe someone who loves the Muse
are all forms of the serpent's head
their God tells them to bruise;

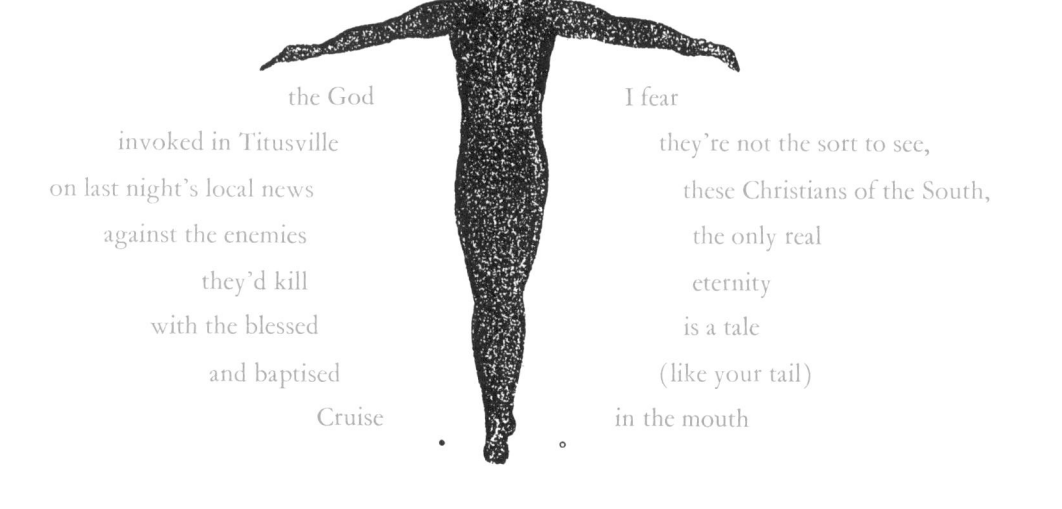

the God
invoked in Titusville
on last night's local news
against the enemies
they'd kill
with the blessed
and baptised
Cruise

I fear
they're not the sort to see,
these Christians of the South,
the only real
eternity
is a tale
(like your tail)
in the mouth

so scared that I mistake
the rattle of my thermos ice
for the angry rattlesnake?
I've started when a pine twig broke
or found I'd only been afraid
of some broken branch of dead live-oak
zig-zagged with sun and shade.
But if some barley starts to sway
against the movement of the breeze
and most blades lean the other way
that's when you'd better freeze.
If you've dragged a garden hose
through grass that's one foot tall
that's the way the rattler goes
if you catch a glimpse at all.
I killed snakes once, about a score
in Africa and in Brazil
yet they filled me with such awe
it seemed gross sacrilege to kill.
Once with matchet and domestic broom
I duelled with a hooded snake
with frightened children in the room
and all our lives at stake.
The snake and I swayed to and fro.
I swung the broom. Her thick hood spread.
I jabbed the broom. She rode the blow

makes the slash and live-oaks sway
I go past the deep-dug gopher hole
where I hope my snake will stay
and stay forever if it likes.
I swear no-one on this land will kill
the rattlesnake unless it strikes,
then, I give my word, I will.
This fire-gap we trim with care
and mow short twice a year
is where we sometimes spot a hare,
a bobcat, snake or deer.
They're off so fast one scarcely sees
retreating scut or tail
before they're lost among the trees
and they've thrown you off their trail.
But there's one who doesn't make
quick dashes for the undergrowth,
nor bolts for the barley: that's the snake
whose length can bridge them both.
I've seen it span the fire-gap,
its whole six feet stretched out,
the wild touched by its rattle tip,
the tilled field by its snout.
Stretched out where the scrub's been mown
the rattler's lordly manner
treats the earth as all its own,

I've let the rattler stay,
and go each day with my flask of ice
to my writing shed this way.
I think the land's quite big enough
to contain both him and me
as long as the odd, discarded slough
is all of the snake I see.
But I'm aware that one day on this track
there'll be, when I'm least alert,
all six feet of diamondback
poised to do me mortal hurt,
or I might find its shrugged-off shed –
'clothes on the beach', 'gone missing',
and just when I supposed him dead
he's right behind me, hissing.
Although I know I risk my neck
each time I pass I stare
into the gopher hole to check
for signs the rattler's there.
I see the gopher's pile of dirt
with like rope-marks dragged through
and I'm at once on the alert
for the killer of the two.
Is it perverse of me to start
each morning as I pass the hole
with a sudden pounding of my heart,

On thy belly thou must go!
I don't think Light is what you're versus
though the Bible tells me so.
I've seen you basking in the sun.
I've seen you entering the earth.
Darkness and Light to you are one.
You link together death and birth.
The Bible has another fable
that almost puts us on a par,
how God smote low ambitious Babel
for trying to reach too far.
From being once your mortal foe
and wanting all your kind to die,
because the Bible told me so.
I now almost identify.
So, snake, old rhyming slang's
equivalent for looking glass,
when I walk here draw back your fangs
and let your unlikely ally pass.
I'm walking to my shed to write
and work out how they're linked
what's called the Darkness and the Light
before we all become extinct.
Laithly, maybe, but Earth-lover,
unmolested, let me go,
so my struggles might discover